This book
belongs to
_____

Farmer Herman and the Flooding Barn

Written by Jason Weber
Illustrated by 344 people
with Kaylinn Strock

BroadStreet
KIDS

Published by BroadStreet Kids
An imprint of BroadStreet Publishing Group, LLC
Racine, Wisconsin, USA
BroadStreetPublishing.com

Farmer Herman and the Flooding Barn

A story about 344 people working together to solve a big, big, big problem

Copyright © 2016 Jason Weber
ISBN-13: 978-1-4245-5318-1

Written by Jason Weber
344 illustrators listed in index
Color and shading by Kaylinn Strock
Layout and design by Jason Weber, Ashley Otani, and Kaylinn Strock
Index design by Joshua Kemmer
Edited by Ginger Garrett

Stock or custom editions of BroadStreet Publishing titles may be purchased in bulk for educational, business, ministry, fundraising, or sales promotional use. For information, please e-mail info@broadstreetpublishing.com.

Printed in China
17 18 19 20 5 4 3 2

Dedicated to every child who needs a permanent place to call home
and to the tireless advocates they inspire.

*"I have given them the glory you gave me, so they may be one
as we are one. I am in them and you are in me. May they
experience such perfect unity that the world will know that you
sent me and that you love them as much as you love me."*

Jesus' prayer the night before he was crucified
John 17:22–23 NLT

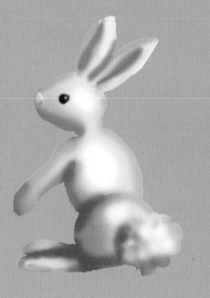

Farmer Herman had a fantastic farm.

He had some amazing animals
and a lovely piece of land ...

... but he had a barn with a **big, big, big** problem.

You see, Farmer Herman's barn was at the bottom of a hill. When it rained, the water would run down the hill and flood the barn.

When the water would flood the barn, it would fill it **way up high** so that the barn couldn't be used for anything.

If Farmer Herman had needed an indoor swimming pool, he would have been all set. However, he did not need an indoor swimming pool. He needed a barn. And a barn with a bunch of water in it just wouldn't do.

Farmer Herman's
Pool Rules

- No stampeding
- No hay in pool area
- Horseplay is encouraged

If you were Farmer Herman, what would **YOU** do?

You could drop a highly-trained team of fluffy parachuting sheep to soak up the water. (Sheep *look* like they could soak up water.)

But you know...

That would be silly. Everyone knows that if you leave a pile of soggy sheep sitting around for too long, they can get moldy. Frank the rooster is allergic to mold. Frank thinks we should skip the sheep idea.

I know!

You could buy a herd of pet elephants that could suck up all the water with their long trunks and shoot it out.

But I guess that would also be silly. Everyone knows that if you have a barn, you have to be willing to put up with some mice. And elephants **don't** like mice.

Wait ... of course!

You could get a bunch of buckets and just scoop the water out.

But that's silly too because the last time we got out the buckets, the cats kept using them as boats. You could try asking them not to do this, but let's be honest ... you can't reason with a cat.

Here's an idea!

You could get 344 friends to come over and help you pick up the barn and move it to a place where there is no more water.

Now that is REALLY silly.
Let me just tell you how
silly that is. It is SOOO
silly because ...

Now wait a minute ...

wait

just

a

minute!

That just might work!

Farmer Herman and his son Farmer Mike thought it was silly at first too. But then they thought about it. Farmer Mike went out to the barn and started measuring and counting.

He counted up all the boards in the whole barn.
He added up their weight and figured out that
the barn weighed over

16,000 pounds!

Now 16,000 pounds is **really, really, really** heavy.

That is heavier than 75 pudgy pigs.

100 150 250

It is heavier than 6,000 phone books.
(Ask an adult what those are.)

However, Farmer Herman and Farmer Mike figured out that 344 friends all working together could lift something that is 16,000 pounds ... like a barn for example.

So they went to work. They crisscrossed metal bars through the barn so that it would not fall apart when they picked it up. The bars also made great handles!

After a lot of planning, a lot of work, and a lot of math, the day to move the barn finally came.

The Daily Gazette

July 30, 1988

It's Time to Move the Barn!

Lions Finally Find Their Place in Childrens Book About a Farm

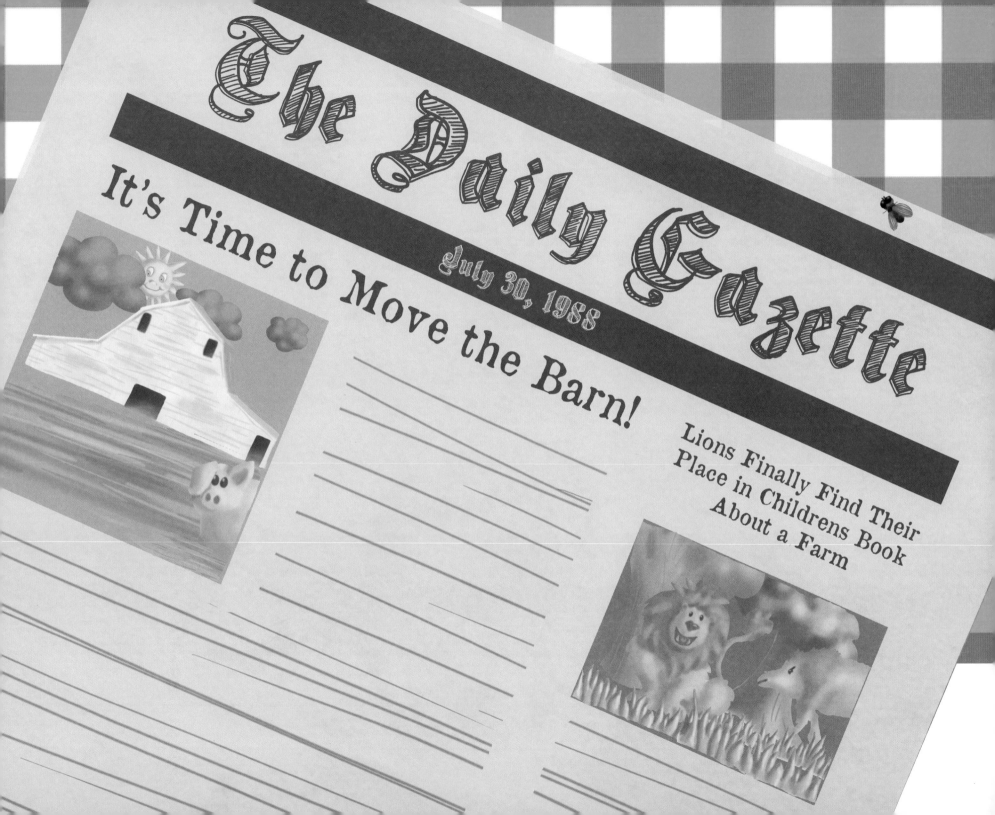

On one July morning, 344 people showed up to move the barn and 4,000 people came to watch! Farmer Herman used a microphone and a loud speaker to help everyone know what they should do.

Everybody got in their positions. They reached
down at the same time and grabbed a handle.
When Farmer Herman told them to lift up on
their handles, guess what happened?

The barn came

up off the ground!

Everyone that had come to watch couldn't believe their eyes. After all, they had never seen people pick up a barn before. Everyone cheered!

When Farmer Herman asked his 344 friends to start carrying the barn up the hill, guess what happened then?

They did just what Farmer Herman said, and the barn started slowly moving ...

up ...

up ...

up ...

... up the hill!

The barn had a new spot on the farm.
It was dry. It was perfect.

And it only happened because Farmer Herman
was willing to try something **really** silly and
do it together with 344 of his friends.

If you were to ask Farmer Herman how someone like you could accomplish something so big and SO silly together with a bunch of your friends, do you know what he would tell you?

He'd say,

"Go for it."

Hey ... Wait just a minute!

This book isn't done yet. There is still one drawing missing ... **yours!**
Draw your favorite animal in the space below.

#344

Now the book is done.
And we did it ... together.

Dear Friend,

Thank you so much for reading *Farmer Herman and the Flooding Barn*. Your purchase is directly helping to equip communities to work together to care for kids and families in foster care. What you just read is based on a true story. Herman and Donna Ostry moved to a farm outside of Bruno, Nebraska in 1981. Their barn, which had been built in 1928, flooded on a regular basis. In fact, on at least one occasion, there was 29 inches of standing water.

After considering the expensive option of having a professional company move the barn, Herman made an offhand comment at dinner one night. "If we just had enough people, we could pick it up and move it." Everyone laughed.

Herman's son Mike went out over the next few days and started doing some calculations. He counted every board and knew the approximate weight of each one. He calculated that the barn weighed over 16,000 pounds and decided they would need to build a steel grid for stability that would add another 3,000 pounds. He figured that if they had 344 people who each lifted 55 pounds, in theory, the barn could be moved.

The town of Bruno (population 143 at the time) had a centennial coming up, so Herman and Mike went to the committee and pitched the idea of making the barn-moving a part of the centennial celebration.

On July 30, 1988, 344 people came to move the barn … and 4,000 others from 11 states showed up to watch.

Following Herman's careful instructions on the loudspeaker, these 344 souls lifted the barn off the ground to the raucous cheers of thousands of onlookers. They carried the barn 115 feet to the south up 6 feet of elevation, turned it 90 degrees, and set it back down. It took about 20 minutes.

We face many difficult problems in our world today and anyone trying to address those problems could learn a lot from the good folks of Bruno, Nebraska.

One of the biggest problems currently facing us in the USA is that at the time of publication there are more than 400,000 children in our foster care system and more than 100,000 of them are simply waiting to be adopted. These are children, who through no fault of their own, have been abused and neglected and now find themselves without a permanent family.

When it comes to foster care, our barn is flooding.

We have more kids than families in our foster care system, and there are more children entering every day. Traditionally, we have taken a "bucket approach" to this problem. We tell ourselves that we just need a few more buckets (a few more families, a little more funding, and some extra workers). We think that if we scoop out the water faster, things will get better. The truth is that using buckets will make the barn less wet, but it will never be dry. Using the bucket approach in foster care means there will be *fewer* kids in care, but there will still be kids without permanent families. We don't need a few less kids waiting for families. We need *no* kids waiting for families. We are going to need to move the barn.

Moving the barn to dry ground in this case means providing *more than enough* for kids and families in foster care:
- *More than enough* foster homes for every child in care to have an ideal placement
- *More than enough* adoptive homes for every waiting child to have a family
- *More than enough* help for biological families who are trying to stay together and trying to get back together
- *More than enough* support for foster, adoptive, and biological families

The Christian Alliance for Orphans' National Foster Care Initiative is working to gather the individuals, churches, and organizations necessary to work together in unity to move the barn. We are looking for people willing to jump in, grab a handle, and lift. We believe we will see a day when there will be *more than enough* for kids and families in foster care. It's time to move the barn.

You can play a part in moving the barn for kids and families in foster care.

When most people think of getting involved in foster care, they often think of foster parenting and adoption. While these are huge needs, there are many different ways for you to use your gifts and skills to move the barn for kids and families in foster care. Here are just a few:
- Mentoring
- Court advocacy
- Providing child care to give foster and adoptive families a break
- Volunteering at a camp for kids in foster care
- Providing families with wrap-around support
- Providing case worker support and encouragement

To learn more about the things you can do and the great organizations that can help you do them, visit:

CAFO.org/FosterMovement

About the illustrations

The pictures in this book were drawn by 344 different people including kids, adoptive and foster parents, child welfare professionals, organizational leaders, authors, recording artists, and you! Most of us could never illustrate a children's book by ourselves—just like none of us could ever pick up a barn and move it by ourselves. However, when we do things together, we find ourselves accomplishing things we could never accomplish on our own.

Each illustrator submitted their drawing in pen. Artist Kaylinn Strock colored and shaded each one as you see here.

In the pages that follow, we'd like you to meet our other 343 illustrators!

There are many things to know about each of them, but we picked one thing for each that shows the wide variety of people it takes working together to get big things done!

1
BISHOP AARON BLAKE
Father of 6 "Engrafted" Sons

2
ABBY McCLAIN
Idaho

3
ADRIEN LEWIS
Global Orphan Project

4
AL GOFF
President, Global Aid Network (GAiN)

5
ALAINA HAERBIG
Maryland

6
ALEX WILLIAMS
Age 7

7
ALICEN BENNETT
Arkansas DCFS

8
ALYCE CHAPIN
Arkansas

9
AMANDA GMUER
Hope Fort Worth

10
AMNONI MYERS
Foster Care Alumni

11
AMY CALLAHAN
Idaho

12
AMY KING
For the Orphan Network

13
ANDI GRAY
Safe Families for Children

14
ANDREA WEBB
Alabama

15
ANDREW PETERSON
Singer/Songwriter and Keeper of Bees

16
ANDREW SCHNEIDLER
The Permanence Project

17
ANGELA HOLLAND
Hope Fort Worth

18
ANGIE PARISH
Gladney Center for Adoption

19
ANN MEYTHALER
The C.A.L.L. Arkansas

20
ANNIE SILER
Wisconsin

21
ANTHONY VIOLI
Texas

22
ARIAL KRIGBAUM
Arkansas DCFS

23
ASHLEY BENNET
Illinois

24
ASHLEY ESCUE
Foster Mom

25
ASHLEY HAEUSLER
Whole Child Initiative

26
ASHLEY OTANI
Christian Alliance for Orphans

27
ASHLEY PHELAN
California

28
ASHLEY SUMMERFIELD
Michigan

29
ASHLI YOUNG
Texas

30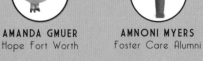
BARBARA RAINEY
Co-Founder, FamilyLife

31
BARBARA ROBINSON
Michigan

32
BARBARA RUEGGER
Switzerland

33
BECKY WEICHHAND
Congretional Coalition on Adoption Institute

34
BENJAMIN PARKER
Michigan

35
BETSY LEWIS
Illinois

36
BILL BLACQUIERE
President, Bethany Christian Services

37
BILL HEAD
Adoptive Dad

38
BOB EISELE
Adoptive Grandpa

39
BONNIE BANKER
Joni & Friends

40
BRAD HUEMPFNER
College Student and CAFO Intern

41
BRANDIE SMITH
Christian Alliance for Orphans

42
BRANDON HOFFMAN
Project Belong Kansas

43
BRIAN DeVOS
Bethany Christian Services

44
BRIAN NUCKLES
Woven Texas

45
BROOKE HAYES
TCU Institute of Child Development

46
BROOKE MARDELL
California

47
BRUCE BARTON
Virginia

48
BRUCE KENDRICK
Embrace Texas

49
BUBBA DOWLING
Kansas

50
CADE VIOLI
Age 8

51
CALEB LEHMAN
Age 11

52
CANDACE GRAY
Buckner International

53
CARA DVORAK
Grandaughter of Herman and Donna Ostry

54

CARA VON TRESS
Prestonwood Church
Texas

55

CARLA HENDRICKS
CAfO African-American
Church Initiative

56

CARMEN GEORGE
Foster Care
Advocate

57

CARMEN WEBER
Age 15

58

CAROL WEBER
Adoptive Grandma

59
CAROLINE COX
North Carolina

60
CASEY WALKER
Lost Kites
Documentary

61

CASSI BAZAR
Arkansas

62

CECILIA WEBER
Age 15

63
CHARIS DIETZ
Buckner International

64

CHARLIE LOWELL
Recording Artist
Jars of Clay

65

CHELSEA GEYER
Executive Director
DC 127

66
CHRIS BOGART
Foster Parent

67

CHRIS DENDY
Foster and
Adoptive Parent

68

CHRIS MAW
Foster Parent

69

CHRISTINE DVORAK
Daughter of Herman
and Donna Ostry

70

CIARAN MOESCHBERGER
Age 7

71

COLLEEN MEDEFIND
Adoptive Grandma

72

COLTON SIMMONS
Adopt Together

73

CONNIE-JO NELSON
The C.A.L.L.
Arkansas

74

DR. CONWAY EDWARDS
Lead Pastor
One Community Church

75

COURTNEY IRBY
Texas DFPS

76
COURTNEY MCCALLEY
Prospective Adoptive
Parent

77
CRYSTAL WILLIAMS
Foster Care Alumni

78

CURTIS ARTIS
Adoptive Parent

D

79

DAN HASELTINE
Recording Artist
Jars of Clay

80

DAN MARTIN
Show Hope

81

DANIELA COATS
Arrow Child &
Family Ministries

82

D.J. JORDAN
Communications
Director. U.S. Senate

83

PR. DAVID ARRUDA
Orphan Sunday
Massachusetts

84
DAVID HENNESSEY
Christian Alliance for
Orphans

85

DAVID VON TRESS
Prestonwood Church
Texas

86

DAVID MCBRYAR
Edgemont Baptist
Church

87

DAVID ARTHUR
Adoptive Cousin
Age 9

88

DEATRA GILLS
Texas DFPS

89

DENA OTANI
California

90

DEBBIE CROFT
Christian Alliance for
Orphans

91

DEBBIE JONES
Parenting Adoptees
Can Trust

92

DEBRA MARTINEZ
Arkansas

93

DEEBRA JENNINGS
Safe Families for
Children

94

DENISE KENDRICK
Embrace Texas

95

DENNIS RAINEY
President
FamilyLife

96

DIANE EISELE
Adoptive Grandma

97

DIEGO FULLER
Recording Artist &
Foster Care Alumni

98

DONALD LEWIS
Kansas

99

DONNA HEAD
Adoptive Mom

100
DONNA OSTRY
Farmer Herman's
Better Half

101

DORIS CLARK
Arkansas DCFS

102

DRAKE BASSETT
CEO. ChildX

103

DWAIN GULLION
ABBA Fund

E

104

ED SCHERMERHORN
Delaware

105

EILEEN MESTAS
Mustard Seed Faith
Ministry

106

ELIZABETH MACPEEK
Foster &
Adoptive Mom

107

ELIZABETH OCCHIPINTI
President
Miriam's Heart

108
ELIZABETH WIEBE
Christian Alliance for Orphans

 109
ELLEN SMITH
New York

 110
ELLIE ANDERSON
Age 10

 111
EMILY BELLINGER
College Student and CAFO Intern

 112
EMILY KASTENS
Age 12

113
ERIN ARANT
Georgia

114
ERIN EBERSPACHER
Focus on the Family

F

 115
FELICIA STONE
Foster Parent

 116
FRED TUCKER
Age 17, Adopted from Uganda

G

 117
GALA GRIFFIN
Arkansas DCFS

 **118**
GARY RINGGER
President Lifesong for Orphans

 119
GAVEN DAUPLAISE
Age 11

120
PR. GEORGE NDAWA
Nairobi, Kenya

121
GEORGE WILLIAMS
Kansas

 122
GINA DAVIS
Annie E. Casey Foundation

 123
GINGER WISCOUR
Texas DFPS

 124
GLENN GARVIN
Royal Family Kids

 125
GLORIA TORMA
TFI & Orphan Sunday

 126
GRACE BURKE
Texas

H

 127
HANNAH GAZ
South Carolina

 128
HEATH PRESSLEY
Pathways for Little Feet

 129
HEATHER ESSLINGER
North Carolina

 130
HEATHER MOORE
Arkansas

 131
HEIDI SAMPSON
Thornwell Home for Children

 132
HERBIE NEWELL
Exec. Dir., Lifeline Children's Services

 133
HOPE LEHMAN
Age 8

 134
MAYA HUDSON
Age 10

I

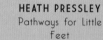 **135**
IVY-MARIE WASHINGTON
Foster Care Alumni

J

 136
JAILYNN SMILEY
Covenant Kids

 137
JAMIE LYNN SMITH
Adult Adoptee

 138
JAMES MESTAS
Age 12

 139
PR. JAMES YIM
Living Way Community Church

 140
JAMI KAEB
The Forgotten Initiative

 141
JAN KEITH
Adoptive Mom

 142
JANET KELLY
America's Kids Belong

 143
JARED BROYLES
Evening News Anchor

 144
JASON JOHNSON
Christian Alliance for Orphans

 145
JASON PEAT
Georgia

 146
JASON WEBER
Christian Alliance for Orphnas

 147
JEDD MEDEFIND
President, Christian Alliance for Orphans

 148
JEFF BROWN
California

149
JEFF JONES
Buckner International

150
JEFF ROGERS
Producer Lost Kites

 151
JEN BROWNING
Washington

 **152**
JEN DECKER
Westside Family Church

 153
JENNA CLARK
Indiana

 154
JENNIFER BELL
Tennessee

 155
JENNIFER BREWER
Arkansas

156
JENNIFER COOK
Foster Care Advocate

 157
JENNIFER MONTEBLANCO
Cactus Nazarene Ministry Center

 158
JENNIFER VAN EE
American World Adoption

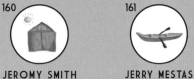

159
JEREMIAH MESTAS
Age 12

160
JEROMY SMITH
Maryland

161
JERRY MESTAS
Forgotten No More

162
JERRY SCOTT
Texas DFPS

163
JESSICA CARPENTER
Together for Adoption

164
JESSICA SCHOOLEY
Arkansas DCFS

165
JILL TOTH
Orbie for Orphans

166
JOCELYN WILSON
Texas

167
JODI LEWIS
Kentwood Community Church

168
JODI TUCKER
Christian Alliance for Orphans

169
JOE FJELD
North Carolina

170
JOE RITCHIE
America's Kids Belong

171
JOHN MCCOLLUM
Ohio

172
JOHN THEISS
Georgia

173
JOHN LUKE ROBERTSON
Duck Dynasty

174
JOHNNY CARR
Author
Orphan Justice

175
JOSHUA JOHNSON
Age 10

176
JOSHUA KEMMER
College Student and CAFO Intern

177
JOSHUA WEBER
Age 7

178
HON. JOYCE WARREN
6th Judicial Circuit Arkansas

179
JULIA SCHULTZ
Age 9

180
JUSTIN BRAZEAL
Foster Parent

181
JUSTIN CLAUNCH
Texas DFPS

182
JUSTIN HEGLUND
Christian Alliance for Orphans

K

183
DR. KARYN PURVIS
1949-2016

184
KAT SMITH
Foster Mom

185
KATE KJELDGAARD
CAFO Intern

186
KATHY OSWALD
Pennsylvania

187
KATIE DEYO
Ohio

188
KATIE OVERSTREET
Focus on the Family

189
KATIE WELLINGTON
Indiana

190
KAY HELM
Tributaries International

191
KAYLINN STROCK
Artist

192
KELLY ROSATI
Focus on the Family

193
KENT HATFIELD
Southeast Christian Church

194
KIM HOPPER
California

195
KIRK WONG
Lost Kites

196
KRISTEN TRUMPP
Global Orphan Project

197
KRISTIN LOWREY
Alabama

198
KRISTIN SIMPSON
Buckner International

199
KRISTIN THOMSON
North Carolina

200
KRISTIN VIOLI
Texas

L

201
LAURA BEAUVAIS
Nightlight Christian Adoptions

202
LAURA DOHERTY
America's Kids Belong

203
LAURI CURRIER
Executive Director The C.A.L.L.

204
LEILA MASON
California

205
LESLI REESE
Northpoint Bible Church

206
LINDSAY MARSHALL
Buckner International

207
LINDSEY FARMER
Sarah's Covenant Homes

208
LISA HENNESSEY
Adoptive Mom

209
LISA LASECKI
Adoptive Parent

210
LISA PRESCOTT
Arkansas

211
LORI BRONKEMA
Kentwood Community Church

212
LOUISE WITCHER
CASA

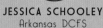

213
LUCY BLOOM
Kansas

214
LUKE VIOLI
Age 11

215
LUVILLA WEBER
Adoptive Great-
Grandma. Age 91

216
LYNZIE BREWER
Adoptive Parent

M

217
MANDY LITZKE
Foster Care Alumni

218
MARGARET TYLER
Nazarine Children's
Leadership Network

219
MARGIE SCHWARZ
Nazarene Children's
Leadership Network

220
MARIN MEDEFIND
Age 9

221
MARK ARMSTRONG
Open Door Church

222
PR. MARK OTTINGER
Fellowship Memphis

223
MARTINA ARNOLD
Congressional Coalition
on Adoption Instutute

224
MARTY BRADSHAW
North Carolina

225
MARY BLACQUIERE
Michigan

226
MARY WELLS
Embrace Texas

227
MARY BETH CHAPMAN
Co-Founder of
Show Hope

228
MATTHEW ODMARK
Recording Artist
Jars of Clay

229
MATTHEW STORER
President
Vision Trust

230
MAYNARD MEDEFIND
Adoptive Grandpa

231
MAYRA VARGAS
Buckner
International

232
MEGAN BUSHMAN
Illinois

233
MEGAN JEDLICKA
Grandaughter of
Herman and Donna Ostry

234
MEGAN MEINECKE
Youth with
a Mission

235
MELISSA CORKUM
Adult Adoptee

236
MELISSA HAYES
Adoptive Mom

237
MELISSA JACOBS
A Home for Me
South Carolina

238
MELODY ROCKWELL
Texas CPS

239
MICHAEL DOURIS
President
Orphan Outreach

240
MICHAEL JAMES
Arkansas

241
MICHELLE DOUGLAS
The C.A.L.L.
Arkansas

242
MISTY KRASAWSKI
Colorado

243
MORIAH WEBER
Age 11

N

244
NATALIE HILL
Arkansas

245
NEMILI JOHNSON
Adult Adoptee

246
NEVILLE BURKE
Texas

247
NICK LYNDON
Restavek Freedom

248
NICOLE WALKER
Alabama

249
NICOLE WILKE
Christian Alliance for
Orphans

250
NIKI BRENTON
Foster and
Adoptive Parent

P

251
PAIGE DAUPLAISE
Age 13

252
PAM PARISH
Author of
"Ready or Not"

253
PEPE TORO
Adoptive Parent

254
PETER PORSCHE
Harvesters Reaching
the Nations

255
PHIL GOAD
Arkansas

256
PHILLIP HAYES
Adoptive Dad

257
PRISCILLA ARTHUR
Adoptive Aunt

R

258
R.D. COGSWELL
President
AIM5 Foundation

259
RACHEL BERNARD
Titanyen. Haiti

260
RACHEL MAW
Integrity Church

261
RACHEL MEDEFIND
Adoptive Mom

262
RANDALL GOODGAME
Children's Recording
Artist

263
RANDY DOLEMAN
The Orphan Care
Network

264
REGINIA HAWKINS
Arkansas DCFS

265
REID BEEBE
Feeding the Orphans

 **266**
RENATA COLE
Arkansas DCFS

 267
REY DIAZ
Executive Director
Orphan Outreach

 268
RHONDA LITTLETON
A Home for Me
South Carolina

 269
RICK MORTON
Author
Orphanology

 270
RICK VALORE
Child Bridge
Montana

 **271**
ROBERT GEEN
Annie E. Casey
Foundation

 272
ROBERT PARRISH
Oakwood Baptist
Church

 273
ROBERTA DAVIS
Tennessee

 274
ROBERTA TONN
Best Neighbor Ever
Age 90

 275
ROBIN BEEBE
Feeding the Orphans

 **276**
ROBYN WRIGHT
Indiana

 277
RODNEY JOHNSON
Texas

 278
RUTHIE TUCKER
Age 17. Adopted
from Uganda

279
RYAN KEITH
Pennsylvania

280
RYAN NORTH
Tapestry - Irving
Bible Church

S

 281
SAMANTHA NELSON
Arkansas

 282
SAMUEL RICH
Lost Kites

 283
SAMUEL WYSS
Age 11

 284
SANDRA FLACH
Justice for Orphans

 285
SANDY GRAY
The C.A.L.L.
Arkansas

286
SANDY RIESKE
Kids Count Too

287
SARAH DAVIS
Foster Parent

 288
SARAH DERINGER
Paoli Christian
Church

 **289**
SARAH GESIRIECH
127 Global Strategies

 290
SARAH KLOTZ
The Twende Group

 291
SARAH MERCADO
TCU - Institute of
Child Development

 292
SARAH NORRIS
Foster Care
Advocate

293
SARAH PHELPS
Foster and
Adoptive Parent

 294
SARAH ROOKER
Christian Alliance for
Orphans

295
SCOTT MOESCHBERGER
Professor of Psychology
Taylor University

 296
SHAREN FORD
Focus on the Family

 297
SHARRI BLACK
Kansas Department for
Children and Families

 298
SHAUNA GOULD
The C.A.L.L.
Arkansas

 299
SHAWN WELCOME
Performance Poet

 300
SHELLY RADIC
President
Project 1.27

 301
SHERRI WEBER
Adoptive Aunt

302
SIENA MEDEFIND
Age 11

303
SOFIA SEGURA
Monterrey, Mexico

 304
SOPHIA WEBER
Age 6

 305
STACY SALLMEN
Indiana

 306
STARLA ABRAHAM
Texas DFPS

 307
STARLA GOAD
Arkansas

 308
STEPHEN MASON
Recording Artist
Jars of Clay

 309
STEPHEN MCCALLEY
Prospective Adoptive
Parent

 310
STEPHEN RIESKE
Kids Count Too

 311
STEVEN ROGERS
Michigan

 312
SUSAN GOFF
Global Aid Network
(GAiN)

 313
SUSAN PORTER
Edinbrook Church

 314
SUSIE ADDISON
CASA of Collin
Country, Texas

T

   315
TAMBRA STAFFORD
Arkansas DCFS

     316
TAMI HEIM
President, Christian
Leadership Alliance

 317
TATE WILLIAMS
GO Project

 318
TAUNYA DEWEERD
Iowa

319
TAYLOR DRADDY
Congressional Coalition
on Adoption Institute

320
TERESA MCCORMICK
The C.A.L.L.
Arkansas

321
TERI FROMAN
Pharaoh's Daughters

322
TERRA TOWNE
Cottonwood Creek
Baptist Church

323
TERRI KING
Michigan

324
TIFFANY WINES
Orphan Outreach

325
TIM SHIRK
America's Kids Belong

326
PR. TIM WILSON
Lighthouse Bible Church

327
TODD WEBER
Adoptive Uncle

328
TOM LUKASIK
4KIDS of Florida

329
TONA OTTINGER
Fellowship Memphis

330
TONJA BOGART
Foster Parent

331
TONY DELILI
Abba's Hands &
Heart Orphan Ministry

332
TREECA DYER
Attorney Ad Litem

333
TRISHA PRIEBE
Illinois

334
TRISHA WEBER
One Community
Church

V

335
VALERIE GRIESSE
Arkansas

336
VANESSA VASQUEZ
Olive Crest

W

337
WALT TANNER
Capstone Church

338
WENDY COSBY
Orphan Institute

339
WENDY KITTLITZ
Focus on the Family
Canada

340
WES MORGAN
Indiana

341
WHITNEY HARDY
Tennessee

342
WHITNEY KING
Washington, D.C.

343
WILL KROEKER
Show Hope

344
YOU!

Special Thanks

We'd like to thank Herman and Donna Ostry and their son Mike whose silly idea has inspired thousands to work together to do big things. Thank you for being silly enough to try it in the first place and kind enough to allow us to share the story for the sake of kids and families in foster care.

We are also grateful to the team at BroadStreet Publishing for their belief in this project and their eagerness to use their platform on behalf of children in foster care. Thank you to Carlton Garborg, David Sluka, Ginger Garrett, Michelle Winger, and the entire BroadStreet team. You have all been wonderful to work with!

Thank you to Jedd Medefind for your encouragement, Ashley Otani for your commitment to excellence, Kaylinn Strock for sharing your gift, and to the entire CAFO team for your support.

And finally, I'd like to thank my wife, Trisha, whose addiction to children's literature was a huge blessing throughout this whole process. Thank you for your amazing ideas, your support, and your help getting all these drawings!